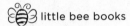 little bee books

An imprint of Bonnier Publishing USA
251 Park Avenue South, New York, NY 10010
Copyright © 2017 by Bonnier Publishing USA
All rights reserved, including the right of reproduction in whole or in part in any form.
LITTLE BEE BOOKS is a trademark of Bonnier Publishing USA, and associated colophon is a trademark of Bonnier Publishing USA.
Manufactured in the United States   LB 0317
First Edition   10 9 8 7 6 5 4 3 2 1

Library of Congress Cataloging-in-Publication Data
Names: Ohlin, Nancy, author. | Larkum, Adam, illustrator.
Title: Vikings / by Nancy Ohlin; illustrated by Adam Larkum.
Description: First edition. | New York, NY: Little Bee Books, 2017.
Series: Blast back! | Includes bibliographical references.
Audience: Ages 7–10. | Audience: Grades 4–6.
Subjects: LCSH: Vikings—Juvenile literature.
Classification: LCC DL66.O35 2017 | DDC 948/.022—dc23
LC record available at https://lccn.loc.gov/2016057764

Identifiers: LCCN 2016057764
ISBN 978-1-4998-0385-3 (pbk) | ISBN 978-1-4998-0386-0 (hc)

littlebeebooks.com
bonnierpublishingusa.com

BLAST BACK!

VIKINGS

by Nancy Ohlin   illustrated by Adam Larkum

little bee books

CONTENTS

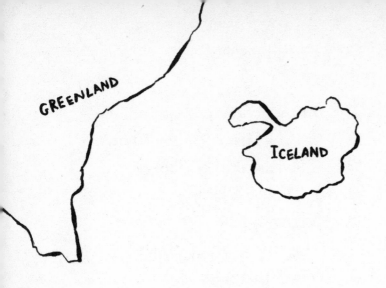

GREENLAND

ICELAND

IRELAND

ATLANTIC
OCEAN

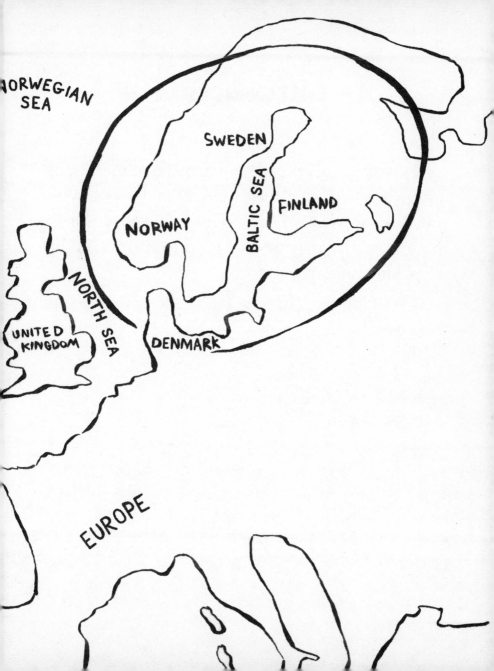

Introduction

Have you ever heard people mention the Vikings and wondered what they were talking about? Were the Vikings real or just legends? Did they sail the high seas? Did they wear horned helmets? Did they have kings and queens?

Let's blast back in time for a little adventure and find out. . . .

A Brief History of the Vikings

The Vikings were Scandinavian sailors and warriors from long ago. The Viking Age started in the eighth century and ended in the eleventh century. "Scandinavia" refers to the countries we now know as Denmark, Norway, and Sweden in Northern Europe. (The term sometimes includes Finland and Iceland, too.) They are also known as Norsemen or Northmen.

The Vikings were similar to pirates. In fact, the word comes from *vikingr*, which means "pirate" in the early Scandinavian languages. They sailed across the high seas in search of adventure, land, power, wealth, and booty (aka treasure). They raided and pillaged cities and towns in Europe and beyond. They colonized some places by force; they settled peacefully in others. They even settled in North America.

The Vikings were never a unified group, though. They also probably didn't call themselves "Vikings," but instead identified themselves by their home country. Some Viking tribes fought against other Viking tribes.

In addition, archaeological studies suggest that a majority of Scandinavians back then didn't actually participate in raids, battles, and other violent Viking adventures. Many stayed home, worked, and took care of their families. Some were merchants who traveled to trade with other lands.

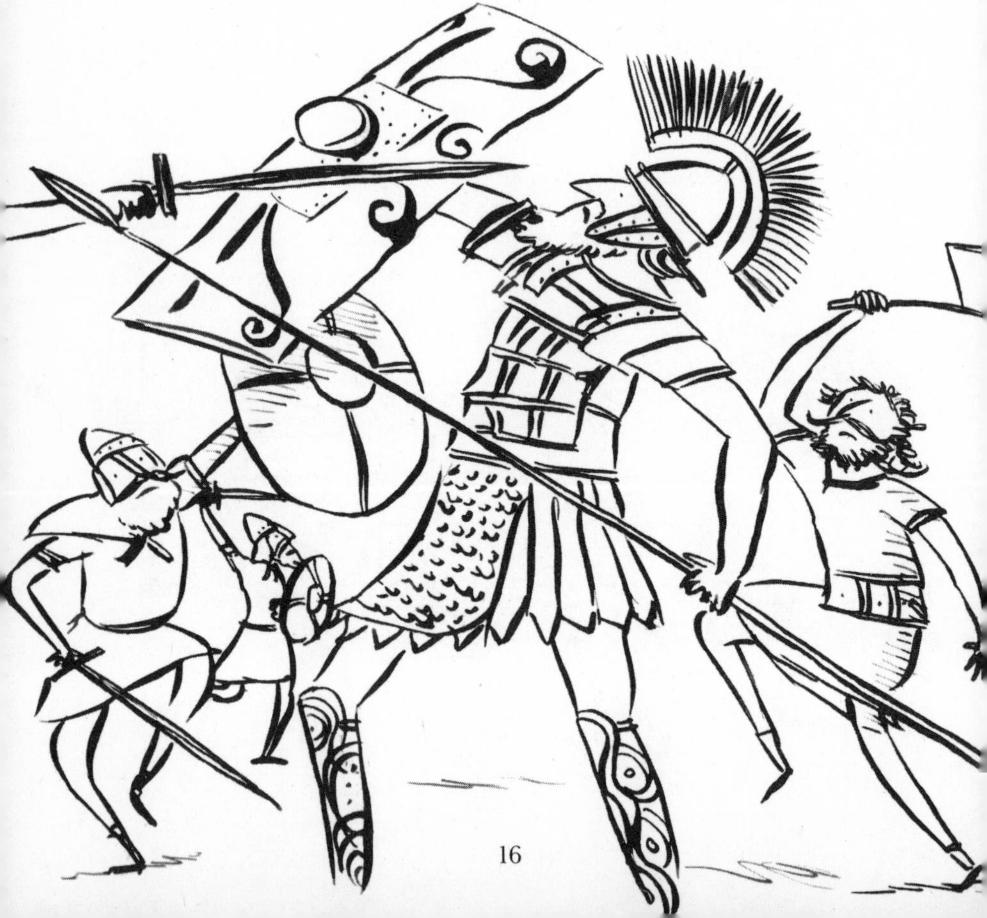

The Rise of the Vikings

Between 27 BCE and 476 CE, much of Europe was part of the Roman Empire, which was one of the most powerful empires in history.

Toward the end of the Roman Empire, Germanic and other tribes invaded the western part of its lands. ("Germanic" refers to certain Europeans whose languages and cultures had common roots.) They split up the empire among themselves. Before, one emperor had ruled over all these lands. Now kings, chieftains, clan heads, and other leaders ruled over a patchwork of smaller territories. This marked the beginning of the Middle Ages, which was a time of great turmoil and change in European history.

The Viking culture emerged out of this turmoil and change. With no central government, laws in disarray, and territories clashing with one another, Europe was chaotic and vulnerable. Furthermore, Denmark, Norway, and Sweden were crowded and lacked adequate land (and good weather) for farming, prompting a desire for new places to call home.

And so some Scandinavians began to assemble armies of warriors. They took to the seas and invaded communities along the European coasts and elsewhere.

Kings, Nobles, and Laws

The Norse title of *konungr* (king) didn't mean the same thing as it does today. A king back then was the head of a tribal community. He could become king and stay king only if his people wanted him.

Next in rank after king were *jarls* (nobles), who were powerful landowners.

Each tribal community had a *thing* (assembly). The members of a thing made laws and also acted as a court. Only landowners could be members of a thing.

Before 1100 or so, laws were not written down. They were based on traditions and popular opinions.

A Typical Viking

The leaders of the Vikings were Scandinavian kings, chieftains, and clan heads. They were also landowners and farmers, as were many Scandinavians. These leaders gathered and organized energetic young men who were eager for adventure—and who were willing to attack, rob, and kill helpless citizens in order to acquire riches and land.

Each generation of Vikings trained the next. Boys were taught to run, jump, wrestle, swim, row, ski, snowshoe, and ride horses. They were also taught how to use swords, spears, axes, and other weapons. A boy might join a Viking expedition and go to battle by the time he was fifteen or sixteen.

Vikings weren't always out raiding and pillaging, though. Most of them spent a majority of their time at home, taking care of their families and working (as farmers, craftsmen, merchants, or shipbuilders, for example). And not all Scandinavian men and boys participated in Viking adventures.

Survival was a challenge for Viking Age Scandinavians. If a person managed to make it to age twenty, he or she had an average life expectancy of about twenty more years.

Girls and Women in Viking Times

Viking girls and women weren't allowed to be warriors like the boys and men. The girls were expected to marry young—as young as twelve years old. A wife took care of the family and the home while her husband was away fighting battles or having adventures.

But a Viking woman *did* have some rights and freedoms. She could inherit property. She could ask for a divorce, and if the divorce went through, she could get her dowry back. (A dowry is money or property that a wife's family gives to the husband upon the marriage.)

Viking Ships

The Vikings were skilled sailors. They used the positions of the sun and stars to navigate. (They didn't have magnetic compasses.)

The Vikings were skilled shipbuilders, too. Their ships, called longships, were fast, light, and flexible, and they could sail in both shallow and deep waters. The longships were about forty-five to seventy-five feet in length (although longer ones have been discovered). They were pointed at each end, which made it easy to go forward or backward. These points, or "prows," might be carved into dragon shapes. (Longships were sometimes called "dragon ships" as well as "Viking ships.")

The longships used both sails and oars. They had a single square sail with bright colors. Around forty to sixty oarsmen were needed to steer.

The Vikings loved their ships and often gave them names like *Grágás* ("the gray goose") or *Ormr Inn Langi* ("the long serpent") or *Dreki* ("the dragon").

The Viking Ship Musuem

Viking ships have been recovered in Denmark and Norway. These ships and other underwater artifacts are on display in the Viking Ship Museum in Roskilde, Denmark, and the Viking Ship Museum in Oslo, Norway.

How the Vikings Attacked

In the early days of the Viking Age, the men went out on raids in small groups. Later, when they had more warriors and more ships, they went out in larger groups and also sailed farther away from their homelands.

In a typical raid, a longship would show up on the shore of a city or town, usually around dawn, while the citizens were asleep. The Vikings would jump out of their longship shouting battle cries. They attacked their victims with swords, axes, and other weapons. They killed some and captured others. They gathered as much booty as they could carry away.

An expression that described these quick, ruthless raids was to "go a-viking."

Vikings and Slavery

The Vikings sometimes seized women (and young men) during raids and sold them in slave markets throughout Europe and the Middle East. These slaves were called "thralls."

Trading

Not all Viking Age Scandinavians took to the seas to conquer and pillage. Some, like merchants, sailed to different ports to do some (peaceful) trading for goods like herring, salt, timber, iron, grain, and sheep.

The Vikings in England

Danish Vikings, or Danes, first began raiding England in the eighth century. At that time, England was not a unified country but a number of separate kingdoms.

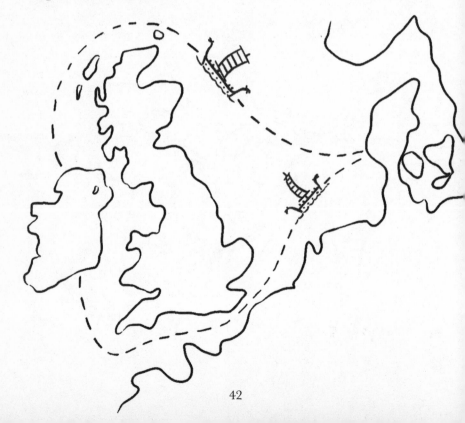

In 865, a group of Danes attempted to conquer England. The attacks were led by the sons of Ragnar Lothbrok, a Viking king: Halfdan, Inwaer (aka Ivan the Boneless), and Hubba. Legend has it that the three men were avenging the murder of their father, who had been thrown into a snake pit by one of the English kings.

The Danes took over the kingdoms of East Anglia and Northumbria and part of another kingdom, Mercia. However, they were unable to conquer the kingdom of Wessex, which was under King Alfred the Great.

Control of England went back and forth between the Danes and the English for a long time. A Danish king named Canute ruled England from 1016 to 1035. (He also ruled Norway from 1028 to 1035).

In England, Canute was succeeded by his son Harold I; his other son Hardecanute; Edward the Confessor (the son of a previous English king, Ethelred II); and Harold II (who was part English and part Danish).

At the Battle of Hastings in 1066, the Normans conquered England, which was under Harold II. The Normans (which means "northmen") were descendants of Vikings who had settled in France. This event is sometimes called the Norman Conquest. The duke of Normandy, William I (aka William the Conquerer), became king of England after that.

Danegeld

During the reign of King Ethelred II, the English paid a tax to the Danish invaders to keep them from invading further. This tax was called "Danegeld."

The Vikings in Ireland

Just as there was no united "England" back then, there was no united "Ireland," either. (Even today, the part of the island commonly known as Northern Ireland is under British, not Irish, rule.) Instead, different parts of the island were under the control of different chieftains or kings.

In 795, the Vikings attacked and burned the island of Rechru (now Rathlin Island, part of Northern Ireland). Over time, the Vikings conquered and created Scandinavian kingdoms in Dublin, Limerick, and Waterford. In the tenth century, several Scandinavian kings actually ruled in both Dublin and in England.

One of the most powerful chieftains in Ireland was Brian (aka Brian Boru). Brian became the king of the Irish province of Munster around 978. In 1002, he defeated the king of Tara, who claimed to be the king of all Ireland; after this victory, Brian considered *himself* to be the king of all Ireland.

The king of the province of Leinster wanted to challenge Brian for his title and also his lands. In 1014, the Vikings (who had been living in Ireland for about two hundred years) joined forces with the king of Leinster against Brian's forces. A fierce battle commenced at Clontarf in Dublin, and Brian's son Murchad led their side to victory. (Brian himself was too old to take an active part in the fighting, and in fact was murdered in his tent by fleeing Northmen.) The Battle of Clontarf marked the end of the wars between the Irish and the Vikings, and Brian lived on in legend as the king who defeated the Vikings. (Over time, the Vikings who remained in Ireland became part of the community, as they did in England and other countries.)

Iceland, Greenland, and Beyond

The Vikings began to colonize Iceland in 874 after taking it away from the Irish monks who lived there. In the following years, many people who wanted freedom from their own countries and governments settled in Iceland, too.

In 982, a Viking named Erik the Red sailed from Iceland to another island that he later named Greenland. At the time, various native peoples from North America resided in Greenland.

Erik the Red had been traveling because he'd been banished from Iceland for manslaughter (the crime of murder). Around 985, he went back to Iceland and told everyone how wonderful Greenland was. The following year, he led a group back to Greenland, which resulted in two settlements there: the Eastern Settlement and the Western Settlement.

Erik the Red's son Leif Eriksson (aka Leif the Lucky) was probably the first European to reach the New World (aka North America)—*not* Christopher Columbus. Around the year 1000,

he and his Viking crew landed and settled in the eastern part of Canada. Leif Eriksson named the area "Vinland" or "land of wine" because of the wild grapes that grew there.

Archaeological Discoveries

In the 1960s, archaeologists unearthed the remains of a Viking settlement in L'anse Aux Meadows in northern Newfoundland (an island off the coast of Canada). They believed this site to be a part of the original "Vinland."

In 2016, an archaeological team led by Sarah Parcak discovered the remains of what may be a second Viking settlement in southwestern Newfoundland. Their findings included a Norse-style turf wall and a stone hearth for heating iron ore. (Parcak and her team first saw the settlement via satellite imagery. She has been called a "space archaeologist.")

Other
Viking Journeys

Between the eighth and eleventh centuries, the Vikings sailed to many other places. They settled in some islands in the western seas, including the Orkney Islands, the Faroe Islands, the Shetland Islands, the Isle of Man, and the Hebrides.

They made raids here and there in what we now know of as France; some formed settlements on the Seine River in northern France. (The Normans descended from these Viking settlers.) Other journeys included the modern countries of Spain and Portugal and elsewhere along the Mediterranean coast.

Going eastward, the Vikings attacked cities and towns along the Baltic Sea. They invaded Russia and moved inland. (Some experts believe that "Rus," which inspired the name "Russia," described the Scandinavian Vikings who settled there.)

At one point Vikings also served as mercenary guards in Constantinople, which today is the Turkish capital of Istanbul.

Viking Religion and Mythology

During the Viking Age, Christianity was the major religion in Europe. Many Vikings were considered to be "pagans" because they were not Christians. (By the end of the Viking Age, many Vikings had converted to Christianity in keeping with the rest of Europe and with the new Christian kings who had come to rule the Scandinavian countries.)

Before Christianity however, the Vikings were polytheistic. (Polytheism means believing in more than one god.) Today, their beliefs are part of what we refer to as "Norse mythology."

One of the most important Norse gods was Odin. Odin was the god of war who protected heroes. He presided over Valhalla, which was a heaven for warriors who had died in battle. Odin was also the god of poets. He was skilled at magic, too, and possessed a horse named Sleipnir that had eight legs and could gallop through the air. Odin had only one eye because he had traded the other one for wisdom.

Another important god was Thor (which meant "thunder" in the Germanic languages). Thor had a powerful magical hammer called Mjollnir that could produce lightning bolts. Also, Thor could throw it like a boomerang and it would come right back to him.

The Vikings were inspired by Odin and Thor, who were warriors, too. The Vikings did not fear death. In fact, death in battle was considered to be honorable; if a Viking died in war, he would be able to enter Valhalla.

Here are some other figures in Norse mythology:

- Frigg: Odin's wife; also called Frija and Freya, her name evolved into the word "Friday."

- Loki: a member of the Aesir tribe of gods, he was a shape-shifting trickster who caused problems for others.

- Balder: Odin and Frigg's son. Loki killed him by throwing mistletoe at him. (Balder had magical protection against everything in the world— except for mistletoe.)

- Njǫrd: a sea god.

- Freyr: son of Njǫrd and ruler of sunshine, rain, fertility, and peace.

- Freyja: sister of Freyr and the goddess of battle, death, fertility, and love.

Loki

Freyja

Frigg

Viking Superheroes

You might recognize the names Thor, Loki, and others from comic books and movies. They are based on their counterparts in Nordic mythology.

Viking Funerals

Vikings buried their fallen heroes with tools, weapons, and other items they might need in Valhalla. Some Viking funerals involved putting the body on top of a boat, setting it on fire, and letting the boat drift out to sea.

Viking Homes

Vikings lived in simple houses, often with just one room and a pitched, or slanted, roof. The houses were made from materials that were available in the area. In Norway that might be pine logs with straw or turf to cover the roofs. Driftwood, rocks, and turf were common building materials in Iceland, where trees were scarce.

The exteriors of Viking houses tended to be plain and unadorned, but the interiors were fancier. Inside, the woodwork might be carved and painted different colors (including gold).

A wealthy Viking probably lived in a compound with many buildings rather than just a one-room

house. (A Viking could inherit wealth and status, usually the oldest son from his father. A poor Viking could gain wealth and status by going on raids and stealing money and treasure, or by earning it through his work, for example, as a successful merchant.)

Viking Fire Starters

The Vikings used an interesting ingredient to help start fires: pee! They boiled touchwood (a tree bark fungus) in human urine and then pounded it until it had the consistency of felt. When the touchwood was lit, it would smolder (burn without a flame) because of the sodium nitrate from the urine. Then the touchwood could be carried around and used as an instant fire starter!

Viking Meals

The Vikings liked to eat meat: mutton, beef, and even horsemeat. (When Christians came to rule the Scandinavian countries, they outlawed horsemeat because it was associated with pagan rituals.) The Vikings also liked fish and eggs. Meat and fish were usually preserved in some way such as smoking, drying, or pickling. They pickled foods in vinegar, brine (salty water), or sour whey (watery milk). Meat might also be baked in hot ashes or boiled.

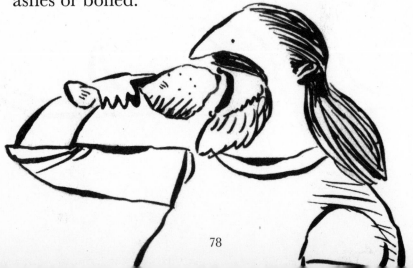

The Vikings didn't have a lot of vegetables. What they did have were mostly hardy ones like cabbage and parsnips that were easy to grow in the cold northern climates. Their only fruits were berries and apples. They sweetened their food with honey. (Some Vikings were beekeepers.) Dairy products included sour milk, buttermilk, cheese, butter, and a yogurt-type product called *skyr*. They also enjoyed porridge cooked in kettles over a fire and bread baked in clay ovens or in ashes.

The Vikings drank lots of whey, ale (a kind of beer), and mead (a fermented drink made from honey). Rich Vikings might drink wine that had been brought over from France.

Camping: Viking-Style

While away from home, a Viking army might stop in a different port each night, anchor, and pitch camp onshore.

The Vikings cooked food on open fires. They ate food like porridge, dried meats, fish, bread, butter, and cheese. Their sleeping gear was made of animal skins.

They tended not to have fires aboard their ships because of the obvious risk. (The longships were made of oak or other wood.) If they had to sleep on their ships, they rolled out their sleeping gear on the rowers' benches.

Viking Clothes

Viking men and women typically wore a long tunic without buttons. The tunic might be made of *vadmal*, which was a woven wool cloth, usually in the natural color since dyes cost a lot of money. Rich Vikings could afford to wear bright colors and patterns and stripes, though. The tunics might be fastened with brooches (pins) and belts. Cloaks could be worn over the tunics.

Viking men might wear sleeveless tunics so they could display their big muscles and gold arm rings. Animal skins and furs kept Vikings warm in the cold weather.

Young Viking women and wealthy Viking men wore their hair long and with a band around the forehead. The band was sometimes made of gold.

Contrary to belief, Viking men did not wear helmets with horns. Their helmets were likely simple round caps constructed from iron or leather, with guards to protect the nose and eyes. The horned helmet myth probably came from artists in the nineteenth century, as well as Richard Wagner's cycle of four "music dramas" (Wagner used this term to describe his works instead of "opera"), *The Ring of the Nibelung*, which is about the Norse gods.

Were the Vikings Stinky?

Likely not! They took baths at least once a week, which is way more often than other Europeans of that time. They also took dips in hot springs, which are like nature's bathtubs.

The Vikings had other good grooming habits, too. Archaeologists have dug up Viking grooming accessories (made from animal bones and antlers) like combs, tweezers, razors, and even ear cleaners.

Viking Education

There were no Viking schools. Instead, children were given lessons at home by a parent or other adult. They were taught how to sing, compose and recite poems, and tell (and retell) stories, too. Girls were also taught domestic skills: cooking, bread making, cheese making, washing, sewing, knitting, spinning, weaving, dyeing, embroidering, and so forth.

Most boys (and some girls) learned to read and cut runes. Runes were the letters of the ancient runic alphabet, called *futhark*, which dates from around the third century to the sixteenth or seventeenth century. The term *rune* also applies to the stones upon which the letters were etched.

Viking Arts and Crafts

The Vikings were extremely talented artists and craftsmen. They liked working with wood, stone, and metals (like gold, silver, bronze, and iron), and they were excellent spinners and weavers, too. Viking jewelry, tapestries, furniture, and other creations might include design elements like animals, scenes from mythology, and inscriptions written in runes.

The Icelandic Sagas

How do we know about the history of the Vikings? The Vikings loved to tell tales about their lives and adventures, but they did not leave written records.

Fortunately, around the eleventh century, some Icelanders began writing accounts of their country's past and about Scandinavian history in general. These accounts, called sagas, included information about the Vikings that had been passed down (and passed around) through oral storytelling. The word "saga" comes from the Icelandic word for "story."

For example, an Icelandic priest named Saemundr Frode Sigfússon wrote a saga called *History of the Kings of Norway*. Another priest named Ari Thorgilsson the Learned wrote a saga called *The Book of the Icelanders*; its subjects included the settlement of Iceland, Greenland, and Vinland. Many other writers, including Norwegian writers, followed suit.

Edda

One of the most famous works of ancient Icelandic literature is the *Edda*, which is actually split into two works: the *Prose Edda* (aka the *Younger Edda*) and the *Poetic Edda* (aka the *Elder Edda*). The *Edda* originates from the thirteenth century, although it includes writings from much earlier. It contains poems, stories, instructions, and more regarding Norse mythology, heroes, gods, and other subjects.

In one Eddic poem, "Thrymskvida," a giant named Thrym steals Thor's magical hammer and

 will only return it if he can have the goddess Freyja as his wife. Thor responds by disguising himself as a bride, showing up to the wedding (in the land of giants), and consuming an ox, eight salmon, and three vessels of mead!

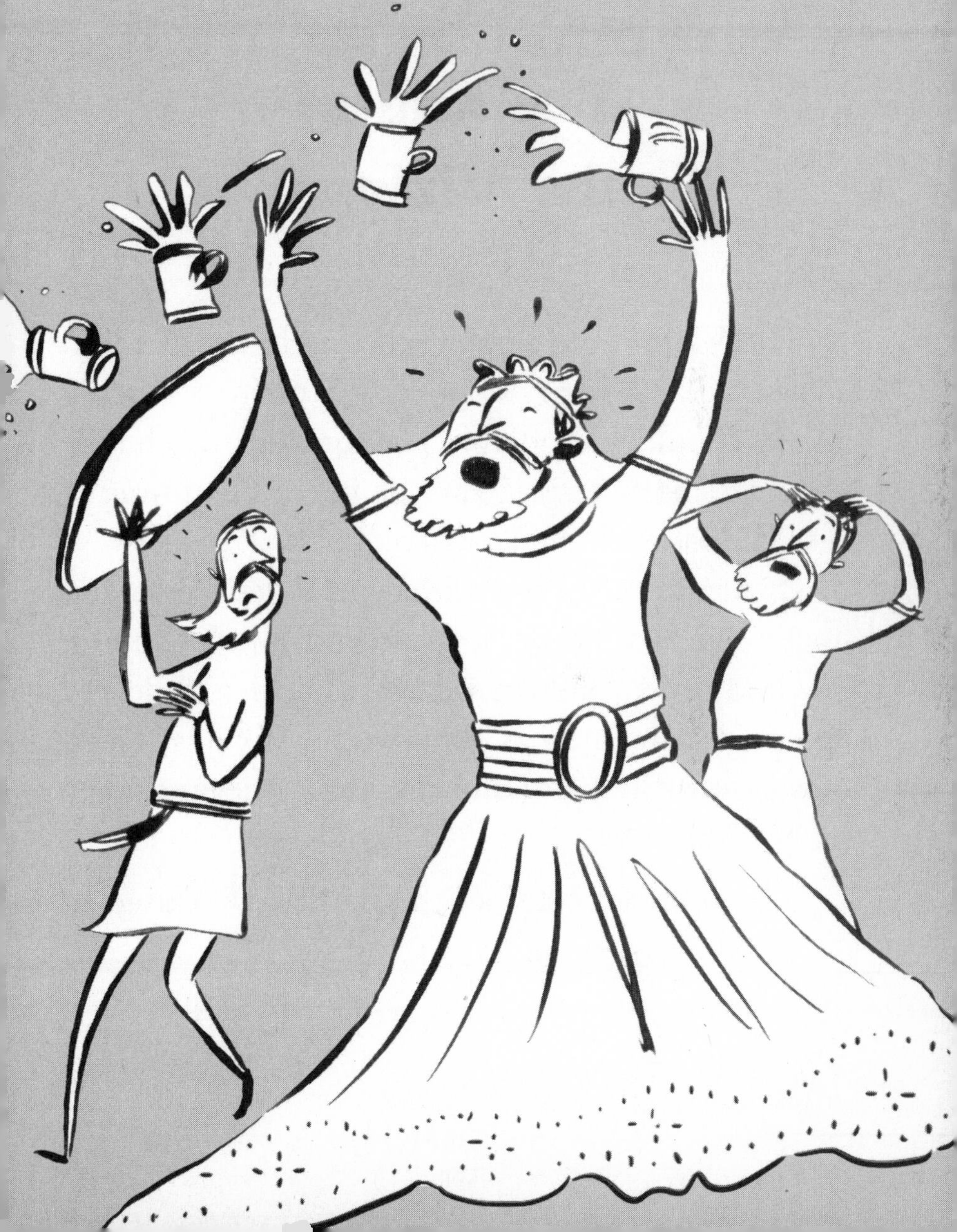

The End of the Vikings

The Viking Age came to an end in the eleventh century. The Vikings stopped organizing seafaring armies to raid and pillage. The turmoil and change that had characterized Europe in the beginning of the Middle Ages had passed. In their place were newly formed countries with centralized leadership (including Denmark, Norway, and Sweden), more law and order, and organized militaries to defend against Viking attacks. And so the Vikings settled down, either in their homelands or in the lands they had conquered.

Some experts consider the Battle of Hastings in 1066 to be the end of the Viking Age.

The Last Viking Chief?

Olaf II Haraldsson may have been the last of the Viking chiefs. Before he became king of Norway in 1015, he was a fierce Viking warrior who fought in the Baltic region. He also fought against the English from 1009 to 1011 (although he sided with

the English king Ethelred II against the Danes in 1013). Brought up as a pagan, Olaf became a Christian and worked to spread the acceptance of Christianity throughout Norway. He was canonized (declared to be a saint) in 1031 and is known as "St. Olaf." Today, he is the patron saint of Norway.

The Legacy of the Vikings

A major legacy of the Vikings is the English language. Because of the Vikings' role in England's history, English contains many, many words of Norse origin (like "husband," "happy," "ugly," "dirt," "anger," "club," "berserk" . . . and "Thursday," which comes from "Thor's day.")

The national assembly is another legacy of the Vikings. A national assembly is a law-making body that represents the citizens of a country. Iceland

formed a true national assembly in 930, even though it was not its own country back then; there were so many different immigrants from so many different

places that it needed one centralized body to make decisions for everyone. This national assembly was called the Althing. (The Althing is distinct from a thing, which is a smaller community assembly.) Today, the Althing, which still exists, is the oldest national assembly in history.

Well, it's been a great adventure. Good-bye, Vikings!

Where to next?

Also available:

Selected Bibliography

The Cambridge History of Scandinavia: Volume 1, ed. Knut Helle, Cambridge University Press, 2003.

Encyclopedia Britannica Online, Britannica.com

Encyclopedia Britannica Kids Online, Britannica.kids.com

History Online, http://www.history.com/news/ask-history/did-vikings-really-wear-horned-helmets

History Online, http://www.history.com/news/history-lists/10-things-you-may-not-know-about-the-vikings

"The Icelandic Althing: Dawn of Parliamentary Democracy" by Jesse Byock, from Heritage and *Identity: Shaping the Nations of the North,* ed. J. M. Fladmark and Thor Heyerdahl, Donhead Publishing Ltd., 2002.

National Geographic Online, http://news.nationalgeographic.com/2016/03/160331-viking-discovery-north-america-canada-archaeology/

Nordstjernan Online, http://www.nordstjernan.com/news/food/5533/

Nova Online, http://www.pbs.org/wgbh/nova/ancient/viking-ships.html

"Old Norse Ship Names and Ship Terms" by Rudolf Simek , from *Northern Studies Volume 13* by the Scottish Society for Northern Studies, 1979.

The Real Vikings by Melvin Berger and Gilda Berger, National Geographic Society, 2003.

Spotlights: The Vikings by Neil Grant, Oxford University Press, 1998.

Viking by Susan M. Margeson, Dorling Kindersley, 1994.

The Viking Age: The Early History, Manners, and Customs of the Ancestors of the English-Speaking Nations by Paul Belloni Du Chaillu, Adamant Media Corporation, 2001.

YaleNews Online, http://news.yale.edu/2013/03/08/vikings-yale-historian-looks-myths-vs-history

NANCY OHLIN is the author of the YA novels *Always*, *Forever* and *Beauty* as well as the early chapter book series Greetings from Somewhere under the pseudonym Harper Paris. She lives in Ithaca, New York, with her husband, their two kids, four cats, and assorted animals who happen to show up at their door. Visit her online at nancyohlin.com.

ADAM LARKUM is a freelance illustrator based in the United Kingdom. In his fifteen years of illustrating, he's worked on more than forty books. In addition to his illustration work, he also dabbles in animation and develops characters for television.